ROOTED IN WEALTH

Rewriting the Rules of Investing

The Feminine Way to Grow a Life That Pays Dividends

Debbie Dobbins

ROOTED IN WEALTH
REWRITING THE RULES OF INVESTING
Copyright © 2025 by Debbie Dobbins

All Rights Reserved

Printed in the United States of America. No part of this book may be reproduced, stored in a retrieval system, or transmitted in any form or by any means—electronic, mechanical, photocopying, recording, or otherwise—without the prior written permission of the publisher, except for brief quotations used in reviews or scholarly works, which must be properly credited.

This book is intended for informational and inspirational purposes only. It does not constitute financial, medical, psychological, or legal advice. The author and publisher disclaim any liability for any outcomes, losses, or consequences incurred as a result of the use or application of any content within.

You are the sovereign of your own life. Trust your discernment, consult with the appropriate professionals when needed, and invest in alignment with your highest wisdom.

For information contact: Debbie Dobbins
https://thedebbiedobbins.com

Book and Cover design by Debbie Dobbins
ISBN: 979-8-9923327-2-8

First Edition: July, 2025

ACKNOWLEDGEMENTS

To the women—both the ones I was born into family with and the ones who cracked me open to find them again—I offer my deepest, most sacred gratitude.

To my biological sisters: thank you for being my first mirrors, my lifelong soul companions, and the ones who taught me, through both contrast and connection, what it means to love across lifetimes. Our bond transcends blood—it is a soul-thread stitched through generations, memory, and mystery. I am endlessly grateful for the healing, the laughter, the forgiveness, and the home we have built in each other's hearts.

And to the six women who unexpectedly activated a soul-deep wound during our time in Playa del Carmen—thank you. Though our encounter was raw, it was also divinely orchestrated. You unknowingly ushered in a profound reckoning that led me back to my sisters, back to my truth, and back to the original wound ready to be alchemized. What felt like betrayal became blessing. What cracked me, also freed me.

In the wake of that pain, grace rushed in. And in that sacred space, I remembered who I am, who we are, and what remains when everything else falls away: love.

To the greater sisterhood of women reading these words—you are my reflection, my reminder, and my reason for rising. We are never truly alone. We are woven together in a tapestry of remembrance, power, and grace. May we continue to heal, to hold, and to honor one another as the sacred sisters we are.

TABLE OF CONTENTS

Acknowledgements iii
Prologue viii
Introduction: Reclaiming the Word "Investor" x
Chapter 1: What Is Investing, Really? 1
    You Are Always Investing 2
    Spending vs. Investing: (Energetically and Practically) 3
    The Motivation Behind Investing 4
    The Unseen ROI 4
    What Happens When We Don't Invest With Intention? 5
    Final Thoughts: Rewriting the Definition of Investing 5
    How Investing Creates More 6
    The Investment Inventory 6

Chapter 2: How Investing Creates More 8
    The Law of Return: Where Energy Goes, Life Grows 8
    Small Investments, Big Returns 9
    Martin's Dinner Table Revolution 9
    Beth's One-Block Miracle 10
    Martha's Literacy Legacy 11
    Alison, the Soccer Snack Queen 11
    Compound Interest Isn't Just for Bankers 12
    Now Let's Talk Money, Honey 12
    The Real ROI Is Mindset 13
    Micro-Investments, Macro-Impact 13
    Your Invitation 13

Chapter 3: This Isn't Your Grandfather's Investing 15
    From Sacrifice to Sovereignty—Reclaiming the Power to Multiply 15
    The Old Model: Security, Savings, Sacrifice 15
    Welcome to the New Model: Sovereignty, Stewardship, and Soul 16
    Fear-Based Security vs. Faith-Based Expansion 16
    The Problem with the 401(k) Mindset 17
    Heather's Story: From Newbie to Wealth Builder 18
    From Pensions to Passive Income 18
    ROI Isn't Just Financial 19
    Using AI & Tools to Get Smart (Not Stressed) 19
    Listening to Your Inner Billionaire 20
    Women as Wealth Stewards 20
    Final Thoughts: From Squirrels to Sovereigns 21
    Reclaiming Your Role as Investor 21
    Final Reflection: Your Declaration of Sovereign Wealth 23

Chapter 4: The Many Faces of Investment 24
    Let's Redefine the Portfolio 24
    The Financial Front: Real Estate, Stocks, Business & Royalties 25
    The Invisible Assets: Health, Time & Relationships 26
    Soul-Level Assets: Creativity, Legacy & Contribution 28
    The Quantum Perspective: The Butterfly Effect of Your Life 31
    Journaling Process: The Many Faces of Your Investment 32
    Bonus Activation 32

Chapter 5: The Ultimate Investment You 33
    The $1 Survey That Rebuilt My Empire 33
    Burnout Is the Overdraft Fee on Ignoring Yourself 34
    Why Every Coach Has a Coach 35
    Leaving the Room That Diminishes You 36
    The ROI of Healing 36
    Why We Don't Do It (Until We Must) 37

    You Are a Living Asset Class 37
    The Inner Wealth Process: Invest in Your Best Self 38

Chapter 6: How Money Energy Works 40
    The Frequency of Money 41
    Scarcity is a Room Without Oxygen 41
    The Difference Between Magnetic and Manic 42
    The Nervous System Is the Real Investment Account 43
    Words Are Currency Too 44
    Somatic YES: The Body Knows How to Prosper 44
    Money as a Mirror 45
    Practice: The Energetic Wealth Reset 46
    Closing Words from the Queen of Magic 47

Chapter 7: Investing and You—Your Wealth Plan 48
    You Are the Architect of Your Portfolio 49
    Aligning with Your Season of Life 49
    Designing Your Custom Wealth Plan 50
    Daily Alignment Rituals 51
    The Energetic Profit & Loss Sheet 51
    The Inner Billionaire Money Map 54
    Your Wealth Portfolio Assessment 54
    PROCESS: Designing Your Wealth Plan 55
    Final Thoughts 56

Chapter 8: A Legacy of Light 57
    What Will Your Investments Stand For? 57
    Success Beyond Self 58
    A Message for the Childless Queens 59
    The Butterfly Effect of Conscious Wealth 60
    So… What Are You Really Creating? 61
    Legacy Activation: Write Your Wealth Intention Statement 61

Conclusion: You Are the Investment **63**
   To Be Continued… 63
   You are the investment! 64
   So here's your final invitation, beautiful ONE… 66

About The Author **68**

PROLOGUE

I didn't plan to write another book.

But after Your Inner Billionaire went out into the world—after the women, the breakthroughs, the tears, the truth—I realized there was still something left unsaid.

See, I taught wealth from the inside out.

But what no one tells you?

There's a whole different kind of investing that no spreadsheet can touch.

And that's why this book clawed its way through me.

This isn't your granddaddy's stock-and-bonds strategy.

This is the fire-your-financial-advisor, kiss-your-pension-plan-goodbye, and stop-waiting-for-someone-to-rescue-you kind of investing.

This is where you burn the dusty old blueprint—the one written by men in suits who never lived in your skin—and build your own damn wealth from the inside out.

Because no one, no one, knows how to invest in you better than you.

Not your partner.

Not your boss.

Not your broker or your banker or your B-school professor.

You.

You are the asset. The strategy. The return.

And baby, when a woman stops outsourcing her power and starts channeling it?

That's when the real compound interest kicks in.

This book is a spark. A howl. A homecoming.

It's equal parts war cry and warm reminder:

You were never meant to follow a plan that wasn't made for your magic.

Let's burn what no longer serves.

Let's build what only you can.

Let's make wealth personal, wild, and wildly yours.

Introduction

RECLAIMING THE WORD "INVESTOR"

Let's get one thing straight right out of the gate:

You, my darling, are already an investor.

Even if you've never touched a stock.

Even if the word "portfolio" makes your eyes glaze over.

Even if you've been told it's not *your* lane.

Too many of us have been conditioned to believe that "investing" is something men in suits do behind big oak doors with complicated spreadsheets and secret handshakes. But that's only one tiny sliver of the truth.

Because here's the real deal:

Every single choice you make is an investment.

That 3 a.m. Amazon scroll? An investment.

Drinking green juice instead of chardonnay at lunch? An investment.

Saying no to the friend who always leaves you drained? A powerful investment.

Letting your nervous system rest instead of muscling through? Jackpot!

The question is never *if* you're investing.

The question is — **what are you investing in?**

And more importantly — **who are you becoming because of it?**

This book was born from a fire in my belly — not just to grow wealth (though yes, please) — but to grow *wholeness*.

We're in a moment right now — maybe you've felt it — where people are waking up. Women especially. We're starting to realize that checking all the boxes, doing all the things, and being "good with money" doesn't mean a damn thing if our bodies are wrecked, our joy is gone, and we're stuck in a life that doesn't feel like our own.

So yes, this book will talk about traditional investing — money moves, assets, legacy, all the juicy things. But even more than that, it's a reclamation. A permission slip. A love letter.

In this book we will are expanding the definition of investing to include:

- The way you speak to yourself
- The way you feed your body
- The way you trust your gut
- The way you build a life you actually *want* to wake up to

You might be saving the planet with socially conscious funds — but are you poisoning your body with food that doesn't nourish you?

You might be fighting for justice online — but are you neglecting the financial stress that's silently strangling your peace?

You might be giving your heart to everyone else — but are you investing in your own becoming?

Here's the truth I need you to feel in your bones:

You are the asset! Hard stop!

You are the account that needs tending.

You are the treasure, the vessel, the soil, the spark.

And when you start investing in *you* — fully, unapologetically, joyfully — the dividends ripple through *everything*.

So no more waiting. No more pretending this stuff is just for "money people." No more sitting on the sidelines of your own abundance.

This is your invitation to reimagine what investing really means.

To make wealth deliciously personal.

To build the kind of life that feels like freedom — in your body, your bank account, AND your soul.

Welcome to the revolution.

Chapter 1
WHAT IS INVESTING, REALLY?

Beyond money: investing is a daily choice of energy, time, focus, and love.

If you think investing is just something men in suits do on Wall Street while sipping burnt coffee and watching numbers rise and fall, let me lovingly interrupt that thought.

Investing is not limited to a brokerage account, a real estate deal, or cryptocurrency purchases.

It's not something that "someday" you'll do once you finally have more time, more money, more clarity.

On the contrary, investing is happening *right now* — in every moment, with every thought, every swipe of your credit card, every boundary you do (or do not) set.

You, my dear, are already an investor. The question is: what are you investing in?

Here's the sacred truth nobody teaches in school—**everything you give your attention to is an investment.**

Everything!

Where you place your energy, your money, your emotions, your time—it all compounds into something. Into a life. Into results you either love or resent. So the real magic isn't in whether you're investing.

You are.

The magic is in whether you're doing it *intentionally*.

Soooo, let's break this wide open.

When you spend an hour doomscrolling on your phone, that's an investment—in distraction, in disconnection, in anxiety.

When you choose a nourishing meal, that's an investment—in energy, in radiance, in longevity.

When you call a friend who lights you up instead of replaying old drama, that's an investment—in connection, in joy, in the version of you who remembers she's alive.

You see?

The moment we start viewing our lives through the lens of investment, we reclaim our power. And this is the heartbeat of wealth—not just financial wealth, but wealth as a way of being.

So no, this chapter isn't about ETFs or annuities or what your uncle thinks about the housing market. We will get to that soon enough.

It's about the everyday choices that shape your destiny—and the ROI (Return on Investment) you're either unconsciously accepting or consciously designing.

You Are Always Investing

Every moment, you're investing in one of two things: your future or your frustration.

Let that sink in.

When you wake up and immediately check your email, you're investing in stress. When you say yes to something that makes your gut twist into origami, you're investing in resentment. When you hold your boundaries like the queen you are, you're investing in self-trust.

And yes, sometimes we invest in chaos because we're addicted to the adrenaline. Been there. Bought the T-shirt. Wore it to the burnout party.

But here's the good news: every single day, you have a choice. Investing is a *daily* practice—not a one-time event. It's not just what you do with your 401(k), it's what you do with your life force.

Time is not just money. Time is breath. Attention is currency. Energy is gold.

So what are you spending your investment on?

Spending vs. Investing: (Energetically and Practically)

Let's talk about the difference between spending and investing, because this is where the game changes.

Spending is when something leaves you with no lasting return. Like buying a fifth pair of black leggings because you can't find the other four.

Like spending two hours gossiping about your ex, again. Like staying in a job that slowly chips away at your soul for a sense of "security" that doesn't actually secure your happiness.

Investing, on the other hand, leaves you better, brighter, or bolder than before. It multiplies. It nourishes. It comes back as friends, money, wealth, happiness, joy, more time and love.

Investing is taking a nap because your body is your temple and your temple doesn't run on fumes.

It's hiring the coach, buying the book, going to the retreat, saying yes to what your soul is screaming for even when your inner accountant is side-eyeing you.

It's not about always playing it safe. It's about playing it *aligned*.

And let's be clear—there's nothing wrong with pleasure purchases. I'm all for shoes that make you strut and chocolate that makes you moan. But there's a world of difference between mindless spending and embodied investing. One is unconscious escape. The other is conscious creation.

The Motivation Behind Investing

Why do we invest? What are we *really* after?

Freedom. Joy. A sense of expansion. To feel worthy. To know we matter. To achieve that illusive ROI.

To feel like our lives are leading somewhere beyond just to-do lists and obligations. We invest because we want to become someone we already *are* deep down, if we could just stop dimming our damn light long enough to remember.

Investing isn't just about ROI. It's about *evolution*. It's about becoming. Becoming the version of you who no longer settles. Who feels safe to take up space. Who dares to create instead of just consume.

You don't invest because you're broken or lacking. You invest because you believe in the seed inside you that knows she's here for more.

You invest because you finally trust that your desires are Divine instructions, not selfish distractions.

And let me tell you—when that shift happens? You stop chasing wealth and start *embodying* it.

The Unseen ROI

Let's talk about the return on investment no one puts on spreadsheets.

- **Intuition.** When you invest in silence, you hear things louder. Your inner GPS recalibrates.
- **Trust.** When you honor your boundaries, you remember you can trust yourself.

- **Clarity.** When you invest in decluttering—your schedule, your kitchen, your mental load—you create space for downloads.
- **Vitality.** When you choose rest, nourishment, pleasure—you literally vibrate higher. That's not just woo, that's physics.

You begin to walk through the world differently. Your energy becomes your business card. Your presence precedes your pitch. People don't just want your product—they want your *frequency*.

Because there is a ROI to joy. To beauty. To being a woman who is not in a rush, not in lack, and not in fear.

What Happens When We Don't Invest With Intention?

Let's not sugarcoat this. When we don't invest intentionally, we pay.

We pay with regret. We pay with resentment. We pay with exhaustion, misalignment, sickness, and sometimes a slow death of our dreams.

When we don't invest in rest, our bodies demand it later through burnout. When we don't invest in love, our relationships atrophy. When we don't invest in our growth, we stay stuck and call it security.

I say this not to scare you, but to *awaken* you. Because the cost of unintentional living is way higher than any course, mentor, or inspired risk you could take.

When you don't invest in your future, you default to your past. And darling, your past may have built survival, but it will never build sovereignty.

Final Thoughts: Rewriting the Definition of Investing

So let's redefine investing, shall we?

Investing is the sacred act of choosing with your energy what kind of life you want to live.

It's what you do with your time, your money, your focus and your love.

It's how you say, every single day: "I believe in who I'm becoming."

And it starts right here, with this page, with this breath, with this next brave choice you make.

Because you are not just a consumer. You are a creator.

And the world doesn't need more spreadsheets. It needs more women who remember their power to *invest on purpose*.

How Investing Creates More

Now that we've flipped the table on the old, dusty definition of investing—and poured some glitter on it for good measure—let's take this one step further.

If every choice is an investment, then *some* choices must yield more than others, right? So how do you know which investments multiply your joy, your peace, your wealth, your health—and which ones quietly siphon your life force?

We're about to talk compounding—of money, sure—but also of *magic*. How small, soulful deposits in the bank of your future self don't just grow... they snowball. Into confidence. Into miracles. Into a life that no longer feels like a chore chart with mascara.

So tighten your crown, Queen. We're about to get into the delicious math of momentum.

➡ The Investment Inventory

Let's get practical—and a little mystical—with a 10-minute journaling practice to activate your awareness and intention.

The Investment Inventory — Where's Your Wealth Going Now?

Grab your journal and answer these questions honestly. There are no right answers—only revealing ones.

1. Where did your energy go today?
List 5 things you gave your attention, time, or focus to. Label each one: **investment** or **expense**.

2. What did you spend time on that drained you?
Would you call that a conscious investment—or a habitual leak?

3. What lifted you up, even just a little?
That's an investment in your vitality. Circle it. Highlight it. Do more of it.

4. What's one area of your life you've been *avoiding* investing in?
Why? What belief is standing in the way?

5. If you believed your future self was watching, what would she *beg* you to start investing in today?
Now, set a 24-hour intention:

→ **What's one micro-investment you can make today that will pay off in joy, peace, or prosperity later?**
(Think: drinking water with lemon, canceling that draining meeting, writing one page of your book, texting a friend who *gets you*.)

This is how wealth starts—not in your wallet, but in your awareness.

Chapter 2

HOW INVESTING CREATES MORE

The Compound Effect of Habits, Energy, and Intention

We've all heard the phrase "compound interest is the eighth wonder of the world." And while that's true for your bank account, let me whisper something even more powerful into your soul: compound interest applies to everything.

Yes, everything!

Every habit.

Every thought.

Every bite you eat.

Every minute you gift to someone you love.

Every choice you make from presence rather than panic.

These aren't just decisions. These are investments. And they don't just pay you back — they pay everyone around you back. Tenfold. Hundredfold. Generationally.

See, most people think of investing as something reserved for brokers, suits, and spreadsheets. But the real magic of investing isn't in the stock ticker — it's in the slow, sacred accumulation of your energy.

The Law of Return: Where Energy Goes, Life Grows

There's an unshakable law in this Universe: where attention and energy go, life grows.

Put love into your garden? You get tomatoes.

Put presence into your kids? You get connection.

Put movement into your body? You get vitality.

Put creativity into your ideas? You get solutions, books, movements, revolutions.

And while the world screams "More! Bigger! Faster!" — the truth is, investing isn't about speed. It's about consistency. Tiny drops of intention, collected over time, that grow into oceans of joy, wealth, health, and impact.

Small Investments, Big Returns

Let's get real and bring this home with some beautiful, everyday stories. Because not all ROI is measured in commas and zeroes. Some of the most potent returns come in the form of peace, pride, and the way your heart swells when you know you're living aligned.

Martin's Dinner Table Revolution

Martin was a busy father of three — the kind of guy whose phone never stopped buzzing and whose emails multiplied like rabbits. His kids were growing up fast, and he could feel the distance stretching with every "maybe later" and "I'm too tired."

One day, he made a radical decision. He didn't quit his job or move to Bali. He simply shifted his work schedule by one hour, choosing to come in earlier so he could be home every night for dinner.

That one-hour investment changed everything.

Not only did he start looking forward to dinner — real dinners, with laughter and stories and the occasional mashed potato fight — but his relationship with his children deepened. They opened up. They asked questions. They lingered after dessert. And Martin? He felt more alive than he had in years.

That's the power of investing your **time** with intention. The ROI? Connection. Legacy. Love.

Beth's One-Block Miracle

Beth who was 68 had been feeling stuck — physically, emotionally, and spiritually. She wasn't depressed exactly, but she certainly wasn't thriving. One day, she laced up her shoes and walked around the block. Just once.

The next day, she did it again.

And again.

And again.

Weeks later, that one block became a mile.

Then a daily ritual.

Then a local 5K.

But here's where it gets beautiful: her consistency and quiet determination didn't just change her life — it inspired others. Seniors in her neighborhood began asking her for tips. She started a walking club. She was eventually offered a job leading wellness groups for older adults, helping them reclaim vitality, mobility, and self-worth.

What started as a single step became a ripple that changed the lives of dozens.

That's the power of investing in your **health and self-belief**. The ROI? Confidence. Influence. A paycheck with purpose.

Martha's Literacy Legacy

Martha never sought the spotlight. She just wanted to help.

She signed up to volunteer teaching adult literacy at the community center. One night a week, for one hour. That's it.

But that hour multiplied in ways she never imagined. Her students didn't just learn to read — they read to their kids. They helped with homework. They applied for jobs they once felt too ashamed to pursue. One man brought tears to her eyes when he said, "For the first time, I read my daughter a bedtime story."

Martha didn't invest millions. She invested **presence and patience**. And in return, she lit the torch of generational change.

Alison, the Soccer Snack Queen

Let's talk about Alison — a single mom who never missed her daughter's soccer games. But more than that, she brought the snacks. The *good* ones. Sliced fruit, hummus, water bottles, gluten-free options — the kind of thing most moms intend to do but forget about when life gets busy.

She never asked for recognition. But week after week, she showed up. Other parents started taking notice. Kids talked about her snacks more than the score. Before long, her story was featured in a local blog, and the mayor surprised her with a key to the city at the end-of-season celebration.

Alison didn't do it for the accolades. She did it because it felt good to nourish her community. And the community felt that. The ROI? Belonging. Joy. And a legacy of generosity her daughter will never forget.

Compound Interest Isn't Just for Bankers

Each of these stories reflects a universal truth: we are **always** investing.

The question isn't "Are you an investor?"

It's "What are you investing in?"

Because energy compounds.

Attention compounds.

Habits compound.

Generosity compounds.

You may think your five-minute meditation doesn't matter. But do it for a year? You're rewiring your nervous system.

You may think speaking kindly to your partner is just being polite. But do it daily? You're building a marriage that glows with trust.

You may think declining one more meeting for an hour of rest is lazy. But do it consistently? You're modeling sovereignty.

Now Let's Talk Money, Honey

Let's bring it back to dollars. Because just like with your time, health, and love — the tiniest financial habits add up in extraordinary ways.

We live in a culture that glorifies big wins: IPOs, crypto surges, lottery tickets. But true wealth? It's built quietly, with calm confidence, not chaotic chasing. It starts with a dollar set aside, a lunch packed from home, a course you buy instead of a handbag.

Investing isn't always sexy. It's not always obvious. But it is always powerful.

When you start directing your money with intention — rather than letting it leak through impulse or obligation — you reclaim your power. And THAT is the return on investment we're after: Sovereignty. Choice. Overflow.

The Real ROI Is Mindset

You can make all the money in the world, but if your mindset is wired for scarcity, you'll never feel rich. So let me say this like the Queen of Magic I am: your thoughts are investors too. Your beliefs are making deposits every day.

Are they compounding your confidence or your doubt?

When you believe that your efforts matter, that your small actions ripple, that your energy has value — you start showing up differently. You walk taller. You say yes to opportunities. You charge what you're worth. And guess what? The Universe responds.

Because here's the tea: attention is the true currency of wealth. What you water, grows. What you bless, expands. What you focus on, multiplies.

Micro-Investments, Macro-Impact

A father who shifts his schedule.

A woman who walks a block.

A volunteer who teaches reading.

A mom who brings the snacks.

None of these people set out to change the world. But they did.

Because every act of intentional investment reshapes the field. It builds connection. It elevates vibration. It says, "I care enough to give." And the return? Our communities flourish. Our bodies thrive. Our souls light up.

Your Invitation

So here's your invitation, dear reader, radiant sister, Queen-in-the-making:

Be an investor. Not just with your money. With your **life.**

Invest in joy.

Rooted in Wealth

Invest in boundaries.

Invest in learning.

Invest in people who see your light.

Invest in the future you dream of — not the past you survived.

And when you do it with fierce devotion and cheeky grace? The world will rise to meet you.

Because you, my darling, are not just a consumer of life. You are a **creator** of wealth, legacy, and light.

So invest accordingly.

Cue crown drop.

Chapter 3

THIS ISN'T YOUR GRANDFATHER'S INVESTING

From Sacrifice to Sovereignty—Reclaiming the Power to Multiply

Let's get one thing clear right now: if the words "investing," "401(k)," or "pension" give you a flash of boredom or a pang of fear, you're not alone. We've been sold an outdated story of wealth that's about as inspiring as beige wallpaper.

But here's the truth: **investing is no longer a dull, rigid man's game of sacrifice and saving—it's a living, breathing, soul-aligned act of self-sovereignty.**

You were never meant to be a cog in someone else's financial plan. You were meant to create.

The Old Model: Security, Savings, Sacrifice

Our parents and grandparents were handed a blueprint: get a job, work hard for 40 years, and retire with a pension (if you're lucky). You put in your time, sacrifice your energy, stash away a sliver of your paycheck, and hope the system delivers on its promises.

It was a model built on obedience and obligation. It relied on employers and institutions to take care of you—usually in return for your time, health, dreams, and freedom.

But let's be honest: how's that working now?

Pensions have disappeared. Social Security is uncertain. The cost of living skyrockets while wages crawl. And yet, many women are still operating under the spell of this old paradigm—quietly shaming themselves for not having "enough" in a 401(k) while swiping their credit card at 25% interest just to keep life afloat.

Welcome to the New Model: Sovereignty, Stewardship, and Soul

This isn't about shaming the old model—it was built for a different time. But now? We're living in a creator economy, not an industrial one.

The new model of investing is not just about money—it's about energy. It's about *what you say yes to*, how you steward your attention, and whether you're choosing from fear or faith.

This is about reclaiming your **agency**. Investing is no longer just a financial act—it's an *intentional creation of the life you desire*. And that life begins with **how you value yourself**.

In the new paradigm:

- Security becomes **sovereignty**
- Saving becomes **stewardship**
- Sacrifice becomes **soul-led expansion**

You don't need a pension. You need a purpose. You don't need to retire. You need to rise.

Fear-Based Security vs. Faith-Based Expansion

Let's talk about the subtle lie baked into the old model: *that safety is found in playing small.*

In that paradigm, investing is about not rocking the boat. Don't take risks. Be realistic. Clip coupons. Trust your employer. Don't ask for too much. Stay safe.

But here's what most people miss: **true security is built from the inside out**, not the outside in. It's born when you trust yourself to create, to choose, and to receive.

Faith-based expansion starts when a woman says, *I am no longer outsourcing my future to someone else.*

And that includes your financial future.

Faith doesn't mean throwing your money at every new crypto trend or shiny object. It means being willing to learn. To be awake. To be wise. To understand the game. And to listen to that quiet inner knowing that says, "This is aligned. This is right for me."

The Problem with the 401(k) Mindset

For years, women have been told to sock away money into 401(k)s, IRAs, or savings accounts that—let's be honest—we don't really understand.

We've handed over the steering wheel to institutions and advisors who don't know our dreams, don't feel our passion, and don't teach us how the engine works.

Let me be blunt: **you are the most important asset in your life.** Not your stocks. Not your bonds. You.

If you're maxing out your 401(k) while ignoring the credit card debt stacking up at 25% interest, you're not investing—you're hemorrhaging. And if you're letting fear or confusion keep you from understanding where your money is going, you're not stupid—you're just under-informed.

But you can change that.

Let me tell you a story about someone who did just that.

Heather's Story: From Newbie to Wealth Builder

When Heather came into my course, she'd never invested a dollar outside of a mutual fund her employer set up for her years ago. She thought investing was something "other people" did—men in suits, maybe. Not single moms trying to keep up with life.

But something inside her woke up. She realized she didn't want to be a bystander in her financial story anymore. She wanted to learn. So she did.

Within six months, Heather began researching companies. She didn't have a finance degree. She just got curious. She found a company that hadn't yet gone public, studied its growth trajectory, and tuned into her intuition. She *felt* the energy of expansion around it.

She trusted her knowing—and backed it up with research.

She invested before it went public. The day it IPO'd, her investment tripled. In less than 90 days, she'd more than doubled her money. Not because she got lucky. But because she educated herself, tuned into her inner voice, and made an empowered choice.

Today, she's a full-time investor. Not because someone handed her a map—but because she learned how to draw her own.

From Pensions to Passive Income

Our grandparents waited 40 years to receive a pension.

We're living in a time where you can build digital products, online courses, affiliate streams, books, apps, intellectual property, and brand collaborations that create income while you sleep.

This isn't a dream—it's happening *right now*, all around you.

But the old belief still whispers: *You have to trade time for money. You have to work hard. You have to suffer for every dollar.*

Let's be clear: **you do not have to earn your abundance through exhaustion.**

We're moving from labor to leverage.

And leverage comes when you **invest your gifts** into something that multiplies.

ROI Isn't Just Financial

I talk a lot about ROI—return on investment—but most people only hear the money part.

Let's expand that.

What's the ROI of:

- Going to bed an hour earlier so you can wake up with energy?
- Turning off the news and turning on your favorite playlist?
- Saying no to something that drains you?
- Spending 30 minutes learning about how compounding interest works instead of doomscrolling?

Every choice is an investment.

And those tiny investments? They compound. Not just in your bank account, but in your vitality, your joy, your creativity, and your self-trust.

Using AI & Tools to Get Smart (Not Stressed)

Here's where things get juicy: You have access to more tools than ever before.

You don't have to guess your way through your finances anymore. You can use AI tools, budgeting apps, investment platforms, robo-advisors, and side-by-side simulations to get clarity on your financial picture.

Want to know what happens if you pay off that 25% credit card before investing in crypto?

There's a tool for that.

Want to compare your current net worth with different income strategies? There's a simulator for that.

Want to get advice customized to your risk tolerance and goals? Yes, even that exists now—with or without a human advisor.

The real investment here is your **willingness to learn.**

Because when you combine knowledge with intuition, you become unshakable!

Listening to Your Inner Billionaire

This is the part most books skip. But I won't.

Your **intuition is your most powerful investor.**

That little voice inside that says, "This feels aligned," or "Pause here," is often far wiser than a spreadsheet.

But most of us have been taught to silence that voice. We've been told that math matters more than magic. That logic trumps knowing. That the world of investing is hard, fast, cold, and masculine.

It's not. It's dynamic. And your heart has a role in it.

When you align with your intuition—and educate yourself—you become a whole different kind of investor. One who doesn't just chase returns, but creates resonance.

Women as Wealth Stewards

Let's say it loud: women are powerful stewards of wealth.

But we've been left out of the conversation for too long—especially women who don't fit the mold. Single moms. Artists. Coaches. Therapists. Caregivers. Rebels. Visionaries.

And yet—**these are the exact women the world needs to lead the next wave of wealth.**

Because we don't just want money to hoard. We want money to heal. To uplift. To nourish. To pour back into our communities, our children, and our creative legacies.

When a woman learns how to invest—from a place of clarity and confidence—she doesn't just grow her bank account. She **reshapes her world.**

Final Thoughts: From Squirrels to Sovereigns

Let's stop acting like squirrels, hoarding bits of savings in fear of winter.

You're not a squirrel. You're a sovereign.

It's time to stop tiptoeing and start creating. Learn the language of money. Reclaim your relationship with risk. Invest not just in stocks—but in your story, your voice, your well-being, your wisdom, and your future self.

This isn't your grandfather's investing.

This is soul-aligned wealth creation.

And it starts with one question:

Where will you place your energy today?

✦ Reclaiming Your Role as Investor

From Squirrel to Sovereign: Your Soul-Led ROI Strategy

This isn't about playing the market. It's about playing your life differently. Use this process to reconnect with your power, clarify your patterns, and create a personal investment strategy that's aligned with your soul.

🔍 Step 1: Spot the Old Script

What outdated beliefs about money or investing are you still carrying?

Example: "I'm not good with money," or "Investing is too risky."

Journal Prompt:

- What did you hear growing up about money or wealth?
- What's one belief you're ready to rewrite?

✏ Write it down:

🔄 Step 2: See Where You're Trading Time for Too Little

Where in your life are you still exchanging hours for dollars or giving your energy away without return?

Example: Overworking for underpay, saying yes to draining commitments, or ignoring debt while "saving."

Prompt:

- What feels like a poor return on your time, money, or energy right now?

✏ Write it down:

🌱 Step 3: Activate Your Intuitive Investor

Close your eyes. Take a deep breath. Ask yourself:

Where is life inviting me to invest—not just money, but my belief, my energy, my time, or my learning?

Let your body speak. Your gut knows.

Prompt:

- What area of life feels ready for expansion?
- What next step feels light, aligned, or exciting?

✏️ Write it down:

📚 Step 4: Educate to Empower

Knowledge dissolves fear. What's one area of investing or ROI you're curious about?

Example: Crypto? Stocks? Real estate? Licensing your content? Paying off debt?

Prompt:

- What would you love to learn more about?
- What's one resource, book, podcast, or tool you could explore this week?

✏️ Write it down:

💡 Step 5: Redefine ROI in Your Life

ROI = **Return on Intuition, Investment, Integrity.**

Prompt:

- What would it look like to get a "return" on your joy? Your health? Your freedom?
- What's one daily action that will start compounding in your favor?

✏️ Write it down:

🪐 Final Reflection: Your Declaration of Sovereign Wealth

Complete the sentence:

I no longer sacrifice my power for the illusion of security. Today, I invest in...

✏️ *Write your declaration:*

Chapter 4

THE MANY FACES OF INVESTMENT

"Diversify or die" might sound like something your old financial planner barked into a plastic cup of stale coffee—but I'm here to give it a fresh, radiant spin. Because darling, your assets are not just in your bank account. They're in your bones, your breath, your relationships, and the way you greet your morning mirror.

Let's Redefine the Portfolio

You've probably heard the word "diversify" thrown around in every money conversation worth its salt. "Don't put all your eggs in one basket," they say. "Balance your risk," they say. But here's the real tea: most people only apply that principle to their finances.

What if we began to see our entire life as a portfolio?

What if instead of just stocks and bonds, we looked at our nervous system as an asset class?

Our marriage or close friendships as long-term investments?

Our creativity, health, and emotional resilience as the compounding factors that yield not just income—but deep, soul-level wealth?

Yes, I'm going there. Because the truth is, we are not one-dimensional money machines. We're multi-dimensional powerhouses. And when we invest intentionally across the full spectrum of our being, we don't just get rich—we become radiant.

The Financial Front: Real Estate, Stocks, Business & Royalties

Let's start with the traditional pillars. They're foundational, but they're not the whole house.

Real Estate: The Original Wealth Anchor

Real estate is a queen in her own right. Tangible, rooted, and often a symbol of sovereignty. For centuries, land ownership meant power—and in many ways, it still does. It offers leverage, appreciation, passive income (hello, rentals!), and sometimes even tax advantages.

But here's what often gets missed: it's also a relationship. With the land. With tenants. With communities. If done with presence and purpose, real estate can be both profit and legacy.

You don't have to be a mogul with 200 doors. Even buying a duplex and renting one side—or investing in REITs (real estate investment trusts) if you prefer a less hands-on role—can be part of your diverse ecosystem.

Stocks: Playing in the Global Pool

Stocks are often touted as the quickest way to grow your wealth (or lose your sanity if you're checking tickers every five minutes). But in reality, stocks—when approached with patience and education—are a beautiful way to invest in innovation, growth, and long-term vision.

You can own a piece of Apple's brilliance, Tesla's rebellion, or a boring ol' utility company that pays you every quarter like clockwork.

But here's my cheeky take: unless you understand what you're buying and why you believe in it—don't just follow the herd. The biggest return on stocks often isn't the money—it's the wisdom you gain from truly learning how markets move and how emotion can wreck even the best portfolio. Emotional investing is real. (We'll talk about that soon.)

Business: The Sacred Container for Your Genius

For the entrepreneurial goddess in you—your business is an investment in your voice, your service, and your sovereignty.

Building a business requires sweat equity, of course—but it also builds creative capital, leadership skills, and impact. And if you do it right, it becomes a system that works for you, even when you're sleeping, healing, or dancing under the moon.

Think: coaching programs, digital courses, physical products, aligned partnerships, and yes—royalties.

Royalties: The Passive Income You Forgot About

If you've got a book, a song, a patent, or even digital assets like templates or courses, you can create royalties. Money that flows in long after the initial work is done.

This is true abundance. It's the echo of your creative contribution sending back love in the form of checks or PayPal deposits. You gave your gift—and the world keeps giving back.

And let's be real, darling: there's nothing quite as sexy as waking up to money you didn't trade your time for.

The Invisible Assets: Health, Time & Relationships

Now let's move into the deeper waters—the assets that don't show up on a balance sheet, but define the quality of your life.

Time: The Original Currency

You can lose money and make it back. But time? Once it's spent, it's gone.

We all have the same 24 hours, but how we invest them makes all the difference. Who are you spending your time with? What are you saying yes to that drains your life force?

Robin Sharma said it beautifully: *"We become the people we have coffee with."* Or, in my words: Your time is either inflating your value—or deflating your soul.

Time investments look like:

- Saying no to what's not aligned.
- Waking up 30 minutes earlier to stretch, journal, or pray.
- Blocking off time to walk with a friend instead of scrolling social media.
- Learning a new skill that can elevate your career or your consciousness.

Every moment invested in what matters expands the return on your entire life.

Health: Your Cellular Savings Account

Your body is not a machine—it's your temple, your transportation, your transmitter of energy. And she's listening. How you feed her, move her, speak to her, and rest her all matter.

If you're burning the candle at both ends, chasing the next income goal while skipping meals and ignoring that aching back—you're cashing checks from an account that's about to go overdraft.

Investing in health isn't just about green juice and gym memberships. It's about:

- Managing stress (nervous system wealth).
- Getting deep, rejuvenating sleep.
- Moving in ways that bring you joy (yes, dance counts!).
- Listening to your body's whispers before they become screams.

Your health returns exponential dividends when honored early and often.

Relationships: The Original ROI

Some say your net worth is tied to your network. I say your soul wealth is tied to your soul circle.

The people in your life are either deposits or withdrawals. Are you surrounding yourself with expanders—people who believe in you, challenge you, inspire you—or those who drain your dreams?

Relationships are investments of time, energy, forgiveness, communication, and presence. And yes—they require pruning sometimes. Not everyone is meant to go the whole journey with you.

Create space for aligned, nourishing, powerful partnerships—romantic, platonic, or business—and your life will overflow with joy and unexpected miracles.

Soul-Level Assets: Creativity, Legacy & Contribution

Let's go even deeper. Because beyond the body and bank account, there's a part of you that's here to do something sacred.

Creativity: The Currency of the Universe

Your ideas, art, expression, and play are not frivolous—they're foundational.

When you honor your creative nudges—whether that's painting, writing, building a vision board, or singing in the shower—you open a channel. That channel is directly tied to abundance. Why? Because creation and expansion are part of the same flow.

Investing in your creativity might mean:

- Taking a painting class just because.
- Starting that podcast that's been whispering to you.
- Playing piano again after a decade.
- Giving yourself permission to suck at something new.

It all compounds into presence, possibility, and power.

Legacy: The Ripple You Leave

We all want to matter. Not just now, but beyond our years. That's the whisper of legacy.

Legacy is not just about building empires or putting your name on a hospital wing. It can be a story you tell your grandchildren, a lesson you teach your niece, or a movement you spark in your community.

Legacy investments include:

- Sharing your story.
- Documenting your wisdom.
- Mentoring someone who reminds you of your younger self.
- Living as a walking permission slip for others.

And that, my love, is immeasurable ROI.

Contribution: The Energy of Overflow

When we give from overflow—not obligation—we create the most sacred form of wealth.

Whether it's donating to a cause, volunteering your time, or simply speaking a kind word that shifts someone's entire day, contribution aligns your soul with something far bigger than your bank account.

And energetically? It's a wealth magnet. Generosity rooted in joy always returns tenfold.

And energetically? Contribution is a wealth magnet. Generosity rooted in joy always returns tenfold.

But what happens when you have nothing left to give? When you're not flowing in overflow—but fighting for your next breath?

Let me tell you something I've never taught from a textbook.

Rooted in Wealth

I've been teaching about passive income and residual wealth for decades—coaching clients, building systems, leveraging real estate, and designing a life where money could flow without hustle. But no strategy, no spreadsheet, no 5-year plan could have prepared me for what came next.

A cancer diagnosis. A total reset.

Suddenly, I wasn't building wealth—I was just trying to survive.

I found myself flat broke. On food stamps. My energy was at zero and my faith wasn't far behind.

In that moment, none of my traditional investments were accessible. I wasn't flipping properties or closing deals—I was lying in bed, staring down a new reality.

But here's where the real investing began.

From that low place, I started doing online surveys. You know the kind—$1 here, $5 there. Not exactly a wealth strategy they teach in business school. But when you have nothing, a dollar is a miracle. And what I came to understand, deep in my bones, is this: I wasn't investing for financial return. I was investing in my capacity to receive.

Every survey completed was a sacred vote for my worthiness.

Every small task was a reminder that I could still contribute. Still grow. Still believe.

And from that small thread of action came a bigger leap: I enrolled in real estate courses. Still in California, but setting my sights on Texas. It made no "logical" sense. But I followed the whisper.

In less than two years, I had moved, gotten licensed, and rebuilt a thriving life—one small investment at a time.

So if you're reading this and feeling like your starting point is too small to matter... let me assure you: the tiniest action can change the trajectory of your life. The first drop compounds. The first "yes" rewires your energy. The first dollar, the first brave move, the first flicker of faith—it all counts.

That's the real face of investing.

It doesn't always look like Wall Street. Sometimes, it looks like a woman, in bed, choosing to believe again.

The Quantum Perspective: The Butterfly Effect of Your Life

I want to land this plane with a bit of cosmic truth.

Everything you do is an investment—not just in your life, but in the entire energetic grid of humanity.

That might sound dramatic, but it's science. The butterfly effect is real. One small action—like a smile, a kind word, or even a new thought—can ripple into infinite futures.

When you raise your frequency, you don't just change your life—you lift the collective. When you invest in your joy, health, purpose, and wealth, you give others permission to do the same.

That is the true meaning of conscious investing. And it's the foundation for the next evolution of wealth.

Not just richer bank accounts.

But richer lives. Radiant lives. Reverent, powerful, magical lives.

So don't just diversify your 401k, darling.

Diversify your love. Your energy. Your time. Your truth.

Become an investor in the whole, glorious spectrum of YOU.

✦ Journaling Process: The Many Faces of Your Investment

You've just expanded your entire definition of wealth. Now it's time to let it land in your own life.

Grab your journal, light a candle if it feels right, and take a moment to be radically honest—with love, not judgment.

Reflection Prompts:
- **Where am I currently investing most of my energy?**
  (Am I pouring into my finances, health, relationships, creativity—or am I running on autopilot?)
- **Which "invisible assets" have I been neglecting?**
  (My body? My time? My joy? My nervous system?)
- **Who are my greatest energetic investments right now—and are they compounding or depleting?**
  (Think: who lifts me, inspires me, drains me, or mirrors my highest self?)
- **What is one area I feel called to invest in more intentionally this month?**
  (This could be a financial move, a health upgrade, a conversation, a boundary, or a creative risk.)
- **If I treated my whole life as a diversified portfolio, what would I rebalance today?**
  (What would I increase, decrease, release, or double down on?)

Bonus Activation:

Write a declaration beginning with:

"I am a powerful investor in the full spectrum of my life…"

Complete the sentence with your truth. Let it guide your next bold move.

Chapter 5

THE ULTIMATE INVESTMENT YOU

Let's get something straight right now: *you are not just a valuable asset—you are the asset!* Period. Full stop. End of sentence.

Before you ever throw a dollar into a stock, a startup, a savings account, or some shiny investment scheme promising 12% returns and a beach house in Tulum, let me ask you this…

Have you invested in you?
Not just pampering and pedicures (though, honey, don't skip those either). I'm talking about the deep, soul-level investments. The hard conversations. The mirror work. The mentors. The education. The healing. The rewiring of your worth so you don't keep overdrafting from your self-respect account and wondering why life feels bankrupt.

I say this with love and experience, not judgment.

Because I've been there.

The $1 Survey That Rebuilt My Empire

I've taught residual income and passive income for decades. I've helped women build businesses, create royalty streams, and unhook themselves from the hamster wheel of hustle.

But nothing—*nothing*—taught me more about investment than a little stretch of time when life knocked me flat on my magical behind. Cancer diagnosis. Flat broke. Food stamps. Body in crisis. Bank account empty.

That moment didn't just humble me. It cracked me open.

And guess what I did?

I started doing online surveys for $1 to $5 a pop. Lying in bed, IV drip in one arm, laptop balanced on my stomach, clicking through market research for pennies. That may not sound like a million-dollar strategy—and it wasn't.

But it was an *energetic strategy*.

What I was really investing in wasn't dollars—it was my capacity to receive.

Even the smallest "yes" to yourself when the world says "you're done" is a *radical act of creation*.

That season taught me that every investment begins with intention. It wasn't about the money. It was about choosing to believe there was still value in me. And from that belief, I rebuilt my empire.

So yes, start where you are. Even if it's one dollar. Even if it's ten minutes. Even if it's just one new thought.

Burnout Is the Overdraft Fee on Ignoring Yourself

Now let's talk about burnout. You know, that all-too-familiar feeling of dragging your bones out of bed while your soul stays under the covers.

Burnout isn't just stress. It's a sign you've been giving without receiving. It's the consequence of investing in everyone *but* yourself.

Burnout is your soul saying: "Hey queen, you've been swiping your energy card with no deposits."

And trust me, no one is coming to refill your account but you.

That's why I say self-investment isn't a luxury—it's *maintenance*. It's spiritual bookkeeping. Emotional wealth-building. The kind of ROI that compounds in every area of life.

Why Every Coach Has a Coach

When I hired my first coach in the late 90s, I didn't even know coaching was a thing. But the moment I said yes, I knew: this is who I've always been—I just didn't have the language for it.

And one of the first things I learned?

Every coach has a coach.
Not because they're broken. Not because they can't figure it out. But because they know something most people miss: the best investment is in reflection, refinement, and evolution.

Having a coach is like having a mirror that doesn't lie and a cheerleader who won't let you forget who you are.

I've spent hundreds of thousands of dollars on mentors, trainings, masterminds, retreats, and sacred support. And I'd do it again in a heartbeat.

Because no 401(k), no IRA, no real estate portfolio will ever outperform the returns I've gotten from becoming *more me*.

I'll say that again for the ladies in the back...

You are your best return!
And guess what? That investment isn't just about business or money. It's emotional. Physical. Spiritual. Energetic.

The version of you that chooses to heal—makes more.

The version of you that sets boundaries—glows more.

The version of you that walks away from toxic patterns, people, and paychecks—*receives* more.

Leaving the Room That Diminishes You

Let me tell you, walking away is a form of investment too.

I've left high-paying opportunities because they felt like soul-debt. I've ended relationships that looked good on paper but drained me dry. I've exited communities and programs where I had to shrink to stay.

Leaving those spaces cost something… and paid me back *tenfold*.

Sometimes, investing in yourself looks like letting go of what doesn't serve, even when it's familiar. Especially when it's familiar.

You don't need to earn your way into abundance through suffering.

You need to *invest* your way there through alignment.

The ROI of Healing

We talk about assets and liabilities all day long in finance. Let's apply that same brilliance to the inner world.

- Unprocessed trauma? Liability.
- Forgiveness? Asset.
- Suppressed truth? Liability.
- Speaking up? Asset.
- Pretending to be someone else? Liability.
- Showing up in your truth—even when it shakes? *Major asset.*

I once said, "If I stop learning, I'm ready to transition." And I meant it. This journey of investing in myself is the reason I'm still here. Radiant. Alive. On purpose.

Every healing I've done—every belief I've released—every dollar I've spent on becoming more whole has expanded my wealth in ways I can't even count.

And it never stops. Not because I'm broken. But because I'm *becoming*.

Why We Don't Do It (Until We Must)

So why don't more women do this?

Because we're taught to pour into others first. To sacrifice. To earn our worth. To save, defer, shrink, wait. We've got entire systems built on the idea that self-denial is noble.

Let me lovingly say: **it's not.**

Self-denial is expensive. The longer you postpone your healing, your voice, your truth—the more interest it accrues in the form of anxiety, illness, resentment, exhaustion, and disconnection.

The minute you say, *"No more. I choose me,"* the debt clock stops. And the return clock begins.

You don't have to hit rock bottom like I did.

You can start today.

Even with five minutes of silence.

Even with one clear decision.

Even with clicking a link to hire the coach, book the retreat, leave the job, start the journey.

And if you're thinking, "I don't have the money to invest in myself," I'll tell you this: the *moment* you commit, the resources begin to show up. Not before. Not later. But *when you decide you're worth it.*

That's not manifestation fluff. That's universal law.

You Are a Living Asset Class

It's time to stop treating yourself like a liability. You are not a risk. You are a miracle. A return waiting to happen.

What's the best thing you can do for your family, your clients, your dreams, your legacy?

Become fully you.

That's the magic. That's the secret. That's the strategy no stockbroker can sell you.

And that's the message of this chapter:

You are your best return. Invest accordingly.

☿ The Inner Wealth Process: Invest in Your Best Self

Here's your sacred workbook process for this chapter. Set aside 30–45 minutes. Light a candle. Pour your favorite tea. Let your truth rise.

Step 1: Personal Portfolio Review
Write down your top 5 investments in yourself over the last 10 years.

- What were they?
- Why did you choose them?
- What was the return? (emotional, spiritual, physical, financial, etc.)

Then answer: *What would have happened if I didn't say yes to those?*

Step 2: What's Draining You?
Make a list of current "energy overdrafts"—places where you're giving with no return:

- Is it a relationship?
- A belief?
- A job or commitment?
- An outdated story about your worth?

Circle the one that feels the most urgent to shift. Declare (out loud): *I choose to invest in my well-being over this drain.*

Step 3: Future You, Funded

Close your eyes and imagine yourself one year from now. She's thriving, radiant, wealthy in all the ways.

Ask her:

- What did I invest in to become you?
- What support did I say yes to?
- What did I let go of?

Write her answers. Don't edit. Just receive.

Step 4: Create Your Investment Plan

Now choose *one* self-investment you will make in the next 30 days. Small or big. Free or paid. Internal or external.

Examples:

- Hire a coach
- Start therapy
- Join a sacred circle
- Book a retreat
- Commit to a daily practice
- Say no to that energy-sucking "obligation"

Write your commitment here:

I choose to invest in myself by…

Then sign it. Date it. Witness yourself. Because this is where it begins.

Chapter 6
HOW MONEY ENERGY WORKS

You can feel it before it ever hits your bank account.

Money.

It has a temperature. A tone. A rhythm.

You know when it's dancing toward you—and you sure as hell know when it's ghosting you.

The first time I realized money was energy, I was sitting at my kitchen table with my head in my hands, three bills past due, a pot of water boiling behind me for dollar-store spaghetti, and a quiet but firm voice inside me whispering, "There's another way."

At the time, I didn't know what that way was. But I could feel the truth of it in my body.

It wasn't about working harder. I had already done that.

It wasn't about saving smarter. I was already pinching pennies.

And it sure wasn't about having the right spreadsheet or the right app.

No.

It was something else.

Something deeper.

That moment—more a soul knowing than a financial strategy—became the spark that led me here. To this chapter. To this truth:

Money is a frequency.

Money is a relationship.

And most of all, money is a mirror.

The Frequency of Money

Imagine standing next to a grand piano, your hand hovering above the strings. You strike one key—and another across the room begins to hum, simply because it's tuned to the same frequency.

That's how money works.

You don't chase it.

You *tune* to it.

And it begins to respond.

Money doesn't live on paper or in digital banks. It lives in the energy you hold, the beliefs you breathe, and the vibration of your receiving field. It follows resonance, not rules.

I've seen women double their income without adding a single offer—just by clearing the shame around receiving. I've seen others lose thousands because they were trapped in proving, performing, or punishing themselves for wanting more.

Money follows energy. Every time.

Scarcity is a Room Without Oxygen

You don't have to grow up poor to carry a scarcity mindset.

Sometimes, you just have to grow up female.

We are conditioned to make do.

To not ask for too much.

To feel guilty for desiring more.

To share, even when we're empty.

Scarcity doesn't always sound like desperation. Sometimes it sounds like:

- "I'll wait until I lose 10 pounds before I buy that dress."
- "Let me just get through this next month, then I'll hire help."
- "I *shouldn't* spend that on myself right now."

I lived in that room for years.

It felt tight, responsible, and reasonable—but it also felt like holding my breath.

When I finally gave myself permission to believe that sufficiency wasn't a reward I had to earn, but a reality I could live in now… everything changed.

Because sufficiency doesn't wait for proof. It *is* the proof.

It says, "I have enough to take the next step."

It whispers, "What I need will show up when I show up."

It anchors you into the energy of *already*. And that energy is magnetic.

The Difference Between Magnetic and Manic

I once launched an offer with so much love in my heart I could barely sleep—not from anxiety, but from joy. I felt delicious in my body, grounded in my message, and unattached to the outcome.

That offer sold out in 48 hours.

I've also launched from panic. From "I need this to work or else." From "Let me add 7 more bonuses and drop the price and send 3 more emails." And let me tell you—the result was never worth the stress.

When you operate from manic energy, you might still make money, but it will cost you something. Peace. Sleep. Your sense of sovereignty.

Magnetic energy feels completely different.

It's the energy of the Queen.

She invites. She doesn't chase.

She knows that money flows toward clarity, pleasure, and trust—not control, fear, or self-abandonment.

The Nervous System Is the Real Investment Account

Your body knows.

Before your brain justifies or your spreadsheet calculates, your body already has the answer.

It's why some "great opportunities" feel off.

It's why that one client gave you the ick from day one.

It's why, even when the numbers said yes, your belly screamed no.

For years, I ignored those signals. I thought I was being dramatic, or emotional, or not thinking things through. But the truth was—I didn't know how to trust myself. I didn't know how to listen to my own frequency.

That's why money work isn't just mindset—it's somatic.

If your nervous system doesn't feel safe to receive, you'll sabotage.

If your body doesn't feel stable with overflow, you'll spend just to release the pressure.

This is why I teach women to regulate *before* they receive.

Not because they're broken—but because their bodies are brilliant.

Because a woman who feels safe is a woman who can hold. Multiply. Expand.

Words Are Currency Too

I grew up hearing, "We can't afford that," like it was a family motto.

So even when I started earning more, I found myself muttering things like:

- "That's too expensive."
- "Must be nice."
- "If I had the money, I'd…"

But those phrases weren't just words—they were instructions.

Instructions to my subconscious. To my cells.

To money itself.

It wasn't until I consciously changed my language that I felt a shift in my field.

I began saying things like:

- "That's not aligned for me right now."
- "I trust the right opportunities will show up."
- "I'm investing in overflow."

These weren't affirmations. They were recalibrations.

They taught my system a new frequency.

They showed money that I was no longer playing in fear—I was playing in faith.

Somatic YES: The Body Knows How to Prosper

I remember once spending $500 on a red silk robe when I didn't yet have $5,000 in savings. My logical mind screamed, "What are you doing?"

But something deeper in me whispered, *"This is an act of becoming."*

And it was.

Every time I wore that robe, I remembered the version of me I was stepping into. A woman who honored her body. Who celebrated beauty. Who didn't wait for permission.

That robe paid me back tenfold—not in dollars, but in embodiment.

When you spend from alignment instead of anxiety, the return is always greater than the price.

That's what I call a somatic investment. It's when your body gives a full YES before your brain makes a plan.

These are the investments that change who you are.

Money as a Mirror

If you want to know how you're really doing with money, don't look at your balance. Look at your beliefs.

Ask yourself:

- What stories am I telling about what I can or cannot afford?
- What emotions come up when I receive an invoice or see a price tag?
- Where do I contract when money comes in—or goes out?

Money reflects your level of trust.

It reflects your boundaries.

It reflects your capacity to receive.

This is not about shame—it's about sovereignty.

When you stop judging your money story and start *reading* it, you become powerful.

And when you become powerful, money pays attention.

Practice: The Energetic Wealth Reset

Whenever you feel triggered by money—too much, too little, too fast, too slow—come back to this simple reset.

Step 1: Breathe Into Your Body
Sit still. Inhale deep into your belly.

Exhale longer than you inhale.

Feel your seat. Your legs. The ground beneath you.

Say out loud:

"I am safe to receive."

Step 2: Identify the Pattern
Ask gently:

"What is this moment reflecting about my beliefs?"

Let the answer come. No judgment.

Step 3: Shift the Spell
Turn your old belief into a new frequency.

"I can't afford it" becomes "I choose to create what I need."

"I'm not good with money" becomes "I'm learning to be a powerful steward."

Step 4: Anchor with Action
Take one small aligned action from this new energy.

Set a boundary. Say yes. Say no.

Make a list. Pay a bill. Celebrate yourself.

Every time you do, you tune to a new frequency.

And that frequency changes your reality.

Closing Words from the Queen of Magic

Here's the truth most financial books won't tell you:

You are not here to *earn* your worth.

You are here to remember it.

You are not here to chase money.

You are here to become the woman who *magnetizes* it.

And you don't have to prove a thing.

You just have to tune in, trust deeper, and take the next soul-aligned step.

Money is already in love with you.

Are you ready to let it show?

Chapter 7
INVESTING AND YOU—YOUR WEALTH PLAN

There comes a moment in every woman's journey where she realizes: *This is my life. My legacy. My creation.* And with that realization, she is no longer content to invest on autopilot—whether that's tossing 10% into a retirement fund she doesn't understand or pouring her precious energy into relationships, roles, or routines that no longer serve her.

That moment is now.

We've talked about money, energy, and alignment.

We've covered the spiritual, emotional, and practical components of investing.

But this chapter—this chapter is your invitation to design your *custom* Wealth Plan.

Not the one your grandparents or even your parents followed. Not the one a financial planner might draft with generic pie charts and market predictions. This is the plan *Your Inner Billionaire* is co-creating with you—one rooted in sovereignty, truth, and joy.

It's the plan that honors your *season of life*, your *intuitive knowing*, and your *sacred desires*.

So let's begin.

You Are the Architect of Your Portfolio

Wealth is personal. Investing is intimate. You are not a spreadsheet, and your goals are not one-size-fits-all. That's why your Wealth Plan must start with one essential truth:

You are the architect.

This isn't about picking stocks. This is about designing a life that is rich in meaning, freedom, pleasure, health, and impact.

Think of your portfolio not as financial assets, but as energetic allocations:

- Where is your time going?
- Where is your love going?
- Where is your attention going?
- Where is your life force being invested?
- And Yes Where Is Your Money Going?

Are you allocating your energy in a way that compounds your joy, your peace, and your prosperity? Or are you leaking energy into obligations, old identities, and outdated "shoulds"?

Because make no mistake: every moment of every day, you're investing in something.

Aligning with Your Season of Life

This part is rarely discussed in traditional investment circles, but it is foundational in my work: **Your season matters!**

A 29-year-old building her career, a 43-year-old mother rebooting her dreams, and a 68-year-old woman reclaiming her magic after burnout—each will have a completely different investment style.

And all are valid.

When I began rebuilding my life after cancer, I was broke, tired, and grieving. That season wasn't about spreadsheets. It was about *survival*. I didn't start with a high-yield index fund—I started with $1 online surveys.

That was the highest return I could create at the time, energetically and practically. But more importantly, those little wins reawakened something in me. A sense of capacity. Of possibility. Of power.

That's when the real investment began.

So ask yourself:

What season am I in?

What is my soul asking me to invest in right now?

What kind of return does my heart need most—freedom? Rest? Relevance? Adventure? Peace?

You don't need to follow anyone else's timeline. You simply need to be honest about where you are, and fiercely loyal to where you're headed.

Designing Your Custom Wealth Plan

Let's break it down. A holistic Wealth Plan includes investments in *five major categories*:

- **Financial** – money, income streams, savings, debt payoff, growth
- **Physical** – body vitality, health choices, movement, nutrition, healing
- **Emotional** – boundaries, self-worth, joy, forgiveness, play
- **Spiritual** – alignment, trust, intuition, connection to Source
- **Relational** – intimacy, friendships, community, mentors

Now ask yourself:

Which of these buckets is overflowing?

Which one is bone dry?

Your Inner Billionaire doesn't judge your answers—she simply illuminates them.

What we're aiming for is *intentional diversification*.

Just like in a traditional portfolio, too much weight in one category creates imbalance. You may be rich in financial resources but bankrupt in joy. Or you might have a thriving spiritual life but a decaying body from neglect.

A Wealth Plan isn't about perfection—it's about **alignment**.

Daily Alignment Rituals

Here's where things start to shift, quantum-style.

Creating wealth isn't about a one-time decision. It's about daily alignment. Tiny, consistent investments that stack up like compound interest.

Here are a few of my favorite alignment rituals:

- **Energetic Profit & Loss Check-In** – Every evening, ask: Where did I gain energy today? Where did I lose it? What thought, activity, or person made me feel prosperous? What drained me?
- **Wealth Journaling** – Five minutes a day to write: What am I investing in today? What's one bold ask or action my future self would take? How did I show up as her today?
- **Sovereignty Scan** – Did I say yes when I meant yes? Did I honor my time? Did I ask for what I needed?

These rituals don't just track your wealth—they *build* it. Because your frequency determines your return.

The Energetic Profit & Loss Sheet

I created this tool as a way to interrupt the unconscious habits that silently rob us of our vitality and abundance.

Your Energetic P&L isn't about money—it's about **vibration**.

Profits might include:

- A nourishing lunch
- 20 minutes in the sun
- A boundary upheld
- A conversation that lit you up
- Moving your body in joy

Losses might include:

- Ruminating over someone else's opinion
- Overcommitting out of guilt
- Skipping lunch for work
- Not asking for support

When you track your energetic patterns, you begin to see that wealth is being built (or blocked) in real time.

Energetic Profit & Loss Sheet

Instructions: Over the next 7 days, track your top 5 energetic 'profits' and 'losses'. Profits = moments, activities, or thoughts that energize you.

Losses = moments, activities, or thoughts that drain your energy.

Weekly Energetic Profit & Loss Sheet

Profits:

Losses:

The Inner Billionaire Money Map

This isn't a planner. It's a portal.

The Inner Billionaire Money Map is your sacred tool for:

- Logging intentional income creation
- Planning energy-aligned actions
- Tracking the seasons and cycles of your creativity
- Aligning your *strategy* with your *spirit*

When I first created this tool, I was living month-to-month, and sometimes day-to-day. But mapping out my energy and intention—before my strategy—changed everything. It trained my nervous system to believe in expansion again.

If you're serious about designing a future rich in time, money, and soul, you must *map it* with love and clarity.

To Access this tool: www.DivineWealthActivator.com

Your Wealth Portfolio Assessment

Think of this like your compass. Your check-in. Your holistic asset review.

Each quarter—or at minimum, once a year—take an hour to sit down with your Wealth Portfolio Assessment and reflect:

- **What are my current active investments in each area of my life?**
- **What's yielding high returns? What feels dry, heavy, or stuck?**
- **What new investments do I want to make?**
- **What beliefs, habits, or relationships am I still "funding" that no longer serve me?**
- **What would a bold, beautiful version of me say yes to this season?**

This is not a punishment—it's a recalibration. A remembering.

Because you were never meant to follow someone else's blueprint.

You are here to create your own economy. Your own ecosystem. Your own abundant life.

Wealth Portfolio Assessment

Rate your current investment (time, energy, money, emotion) and returns (fulfillment, joy, results) for each area from 1 (low) to 10 (high). Then reflect on one action you could take to shift it forward.

Financial
Investment Rating (1-10): _____   Return Rating (1-10): ___
Next Step/Action:

Physical
Investment Rating (1-10): _____   Return Rating (1-10): ___
Next Step/Action:

Emotional
Investment Rating (1-10): _____   Return Rating (1-10): ___
Next Step/Action:

Spiritual
Investment Rating (1-10): _____   Return Rating (1-10): ___
Next Step/Action:

PROCESS: Designing Your Wealth Plan

Set aside 30–60 minutes for this. Light a candle. Play soft music. Make it sacred.

Step 1: Take Inventory

Using the five categories (Financial, Physical, Emotional, Spiritual, Relational), rate your current level of investment and return in each area from 1–10. Be honest.

Step 2: Complete Your Energetic Profit & Loss Sheet for the Week

List your top 5 energetic "profits" and top 5 "losses" from the past 7 days. What trends do you notice?

Step 3: Map Your Desires

In each category, write your top 1–3 desires. What would radical wealth look like in that area of your life?

Step 4: Commit to One Daily Ritual

Choose one simple ritual to begin tomorrow. Wealth journaling? A morning intention walk? A midday body scan? Keep it doable.

Step 5: Choose a Quarterly Investment Focus

For the next 90 days, choose one area of focus. Just one. Commit to being her, showing up for her, and investing like she already exists—because she does.

Final Thoughts

There is no Wealth Plan more powerful than a woman in alignment with her truth.

This is your invitation to stop waiting. To stop defaulting. To stop pretending you don't know what's next.

Your Inner Billionaire has been whispering all along:

You are the asset. You are the strategy. You are the return.

Let the world feel the ripple of your intentionality.

Your future self is already smiling.

Chapter 8

A LEGACY OF LIGHT

Darling, you didn't come this far to stack dollars in a dusty account and call it a day.

You didn't invest your time, your tears, your transformation just to sip green juice on the beach and whisper "namaste" into the sunset. (Although yes, we *will* be doing that too.)

No, my love—you came here to leave a mark.

A radiant, pulsing, soul-level imprint on this Earth that whispers to the hearts of generations to come:

"She lived. She rose. She gave. And she *shined*."

This is *legacy*.

Not the stiff, gray-suited version our culture wraps in legalese and trust funds.

But the living, breathing legacy of **energy**, intention, presence, and power.

The *real* wealth that cannot be taxed, diminished, or divided.

What Will Your Investments Stand For?

Let's get honest, Queen.

What are you investing in… really?

Is it just stocks, bonds, or beach houses?

Or is it connection, creativity, communion?

Is it conversations with your granddaughter about what it means to be a powerful woman?

Is it funding scholarships for girls who've never seen themselves in a mirror of success?

Is it writing that book, launching that business, healing that wound—not because it's profitable, but because it's *inevitable*?

Every investment—of your time, energy, attention, and yes, money—is sending a signal.

Are you building a future aligned with your soul, or one that simply follows someone else's script?

And if your energy is currency (which it is), then baby… *you are the dividend.*

Yes, read that again:

You are *living* as the dividend.

You *are* the return on investment of every single prayer your ancestors whispered into the dirt.

Every act of survival they made.

Every dream they dared to dream, even if they never lived to see it through.

You. Are. The. Yield.

So now the question becomes: **what will you yield in return?**

Success Beyond Self

Somewhere along the way, we got sold a story that success ends when the bank account hits a number.

That once you retire, or sell the company, or get the ring or the beach house or the TED Talk—you're done.

But the truth?

That's just the *on-ramp*.

That's where legacy *begins*.

Real success is what ripples out from your existence like golden rings in a cosmic pond.

It's the way people feel after they've been in your energy.

It's the thoughts you plant in their hearts.

The yeses you dared to give.

The no's you said with love.

The boundaries you kept so you could stay whole.

The courage you modeled when the world wanted you silent.

The permission you gave, just by being *you*.

And yes, sometimes it's the money you gave away or the wisdom you passed down or the business you built—but don't get it twisted:

Your greatest legacy is not the stuff you leave behind.

It's the frequency you lived from.

A Message for the Childless Queens

Now let me speak directly to my women without children.

Because I see you.

I *am* you.

And I know that in a world obsessed with lineage through blood, it can feel like your legacy is somehow...less.

Nonsense.

Your legacy is not bound to biology.

It's bound to brilliance.

It's bound to how many people were set free by your story.

It's the ripple of the healing you chose to do instead of passing the pain along.

It's every woman who stood taller because you told the truth out loud.

Your legacy is *alive*.

And baby, it is *glorious*.

The Butterfly Effect of Conscious Wealth

President Bush once spoke of "a thousand points of light."

But I say, why stop there?

There are **billions** of points of light, and you, my dear, are one of them.

A walking beam of stardust and strength.

A lighthouse on a stormy sea.

A holy flicker of the Divine, dancing her way through time.

And don't think for a second that your choices don't matter.

The butterfly effect is *real*.

Every healed moment, every empowered dollar, every intuitive yes you say shifts the field.

When you stop apologizing for your desires, another woman gets permission to dream.

When you show up for yourself fully, someone else realizes they don't have to shrink.

When you speak your truth in a world that rewards silence, you break the curse.

And the compound interest of that?

Unfathomable!

So... What Are You Really Creating?

Are you investing in drama?

Fear?

Comfort zones?

Or are you investing in your divine expansion?

Your sacred reclamation?

Your magnificent, magical, messily-human contribution to the world?

Because here's the thing:

You *are* here for a reason.

You *are* part of a cosmic design.

And without *your* piece, the whole puzzle is incomplete.

This is not fluff.

This is your *call to rise.*

So let's do it.

Let's crystallize your wealth in a way no trust fund ever could.

✨Legacy Activation: Write Your Wealth Intention Statement✨

Take a moment now and breathe.

Center in your heart, your soul, your womb, your knowing.

Then write your **Wealth Intention Statement**.

This is not a goal. This is a *declaration*.

Start with this prompt, and let your intuition take the lead:

"**I am a radiant force of divine wealth. I invest in _____ because I believe in _____, and I desire to leave a legacy of _____.**"

Let it pour out.

Don't edit. Don't censor. Let your soul speak.

Here's a peek at mine to get you started:

"I am a radiant force of divine wealth. I invest in women's awakening because I believe in the power of feminine energy to heal the world, and I desire to leave a legacy of permission, power, and prosperity for generations to come."

Now it's your turn.

Let this be your guiding light as you build, breathe, and birth what's next.

You are not just investing in your future.

You *are* the future.

And Queen, your light is *limitless*.

Conclusion

YOU ARE THE INVESTMENT

To Be Continued…

Because this is not the end.

This is your beginning.

And trust me—there is so much more waiting to be written by you, through you, and for you.

Let the legacy unfold. 🌱

You've just devoured a book that redefined what investing *really* means. Not just numbers on a spreadsheet. Not just 401Ks, Roth IRAs, or index funds—although those may have their place.

This book wasn't about Wall Street.

It was about *your street*.

The one you walk every day.

The one you pave with your choices, your energy, your desire, your love, your risk, and your devotion.

It's not just about ROI.

It's about *ROY – Return on YOU*.

You are not just *in* the economy. You *are* the economy.

You're the energetic center of your world's wealth ecosystem. And baby, when you stop outsourcing your value to external trends and start investing like your future depends on it (because it does), something magical happens: **you become unstoppable.**

Let's rewind for a second—not to bore you (goddess, no), but to *remind you* of the journey we've just taken together.

We cracked open the dusty old vault of traditional investing and gave it a Queen of Magic glow-up.

We explored the *truth*—that you're investing with every breath you take, every text you send, every dollar you spend, and every belief you choose to hold. Whether consciously or not, you've always been investing. The only question is: *Are you investing in the life you actually want?*

We journeyed through energy, intention, soul, and strategy.

We broke up with hustle.

We kissed burnout goodbye.

We got flirty with faith, and cozy with clarity.

We learned that compound interest isn't just for your savings account—it's for your habits, your joy, your health, and your alignment.

We unhooked from our grandparent's investing model and re-wrote the rules for a new era—one led by sovereignty, by stewardship, by soul.

And at the heart of it all, we remembered the most important truth of all:

You are the investment!

You are the asset. The product. The brand. The empire. The magic. The miracle.

You're not just investing *in* life.

You're investing *as* life.

And that means… everything changes.

You don't wait to be chosen. You choose yourself.

You don't wait for market conditions. You become the condition.

You don't wait for dividends. You live as the dividend.

Because aligned living *is* the ultimate wealth strategy. Every time you prioritize your peace, your pleasure, your purpose—you're investing in a legacy that can't be measured in dollars alone.

Let me be clear:

I can teach anyone to double their income.

I can show you how to invest in stocks, real estate, royalties, and passive income streams until your bank account bursts into song.

But none of that will stick—*none of it*—if you don't invest in the belief that you're worthy to receive it.

If you don't believe you are the one, the Universe will mirror your doubt with delay.

But if you *do*?

If you stand tall in your knowing, own your energy, and align with your divine worth?

You become magnetic.

You become inevitable.

You become a walking, talking, breathing investment vehicle of expansion and joy.

So let me ask you:

🕊 What will you invest in today that your future self will thank you for?

🕊 What belief will you light up with intention?

🍃 What small, sacred, strategic choice will you make right now to shift the course of your destiny?

Because that's how it works.

One choice at a time.

One YES at a time.

One recalibration, one re-centering, one realignment at a time.

And don't think this is about perfection. Ha! No, darling. This is about devotion.

It's about investing as a way of *being*, not a checklist you cross off.

It's about dancing with your desires, listening to your gut, holding yourself tenderly when you wobble, and still choosing to rise again.

This is the era of Self and Soul Investing Women.

We are no longer waiting for permission.

We are no longer outsourcing our futures to systems that weren't built for us.

We are no longer pretending that being busy is the same as being wealthy.

We're becoming fluent in the language of alignment.

We're divesting from fear, fatigue, and false scarcity.

We're reclaiming the sacred art of believing in ourselves.

So here's your final invitation, beautiful ONE…

Choose your investments like your future depends on them—because it does.

Not just your money. Your time. Your body. Your truth. Your intuition. Your rest. Your pleasure.

Your *yes* and your *no*.

Choose it all.

You have something no one else has.

A frequency. A voiceprint. A path. A pattern. A puzzle piece this world has never seen before and will never see again.

Your job isn't to figure out how you fit in.

Your job is to remember that *you* are the fit.

And your life—your beautifully messy, magical, magnificent life—is the dividend that keeps paying out… when you trust yourself enough to keep investing.

This is not a closing chapter.

This is your portal.

Your invitation.

Your divine next step.

Now go.

Invest like you mean it.

Create like you remember who you are.

And live like your wealth is inevitable—because it is.

With glitter, grace, and unshakable belief in you,
The Queen of Magic

ABOUT THE AUTHOR

Debbie Dobbins is not your typical wealth mentor—she's a barefoot revolutionary with a wand in one hand and a bank statement in the other.

Known as The Queen of Magic, Debbie helps conscious entrepreneurs—especially women in their second act—rewrite the rules around money, worth, and wild, soul-aligned success.

After building million-dollar businesses and teaching abundance for decades, life threw her the ultimate plot twist: a cancer diagnosis, a bank account near zero, and a body crying out for a different kind of wealth. But instead of folding, she reclaimed. Through radical self-responsibility, intuitive healing, and the deep feminine art of receiving, Debbie not only healed her body and rebuilt her fortune—she redefined what true prosperity looks like.

Today, she's the bestselling author of Your Inner Billionaire, a sacred rebellion disguised as a book.

It's part spiritual roadmap, part business bible, and all heart. Her work blends Universal Law, quantum energetics, and grounded wealth strategy to help women claim abundance not just in the bank—but in their bodies, relationships, purpose, and power.

Debbie leads transformational retreats, teaches powerful online courses, and guides her Inner Billionaire Circle mastermind with both precision and play. Her mission is simple but revolutionary: help women remember that they are the investment—and the return.

Whether she's hosting a sound bath on the beach, mentoring a woman through her six-figure breakthrough, or dancing barefoot under the stars, Debbie is living proof that it's never too late to rise. Not too old. Not too broken. Not too far gone.

You're not too much. You're right on time.

And this Queen of Magic? She's just getting started.

Learn more and activate your Inner Billionaire at www.thedebbiedobbins.com

www.ingramcontent.com/pod-product-compliance
Lightning Source LLC
Chambersburg PA
CBHW050917160426
43194CB00011B/2450